contents

why breast milk is best	3
breastfeeding	4
father's role	12
in the beginning	14
tips for success	16
common problems and solutions	18
working and breastfeeding	23
wind or colic and how to deal with it	24
weaning from the breast	26
from breast to bottle	26
bottle-feeding	28
washing and sterilising bottles	30
bottle-feed as if you are breastfeeding	32
choosing a formula	33
first foods	34
foods in the first year	36
what to expect	38
nutritional sense	40
mess control	42
eating out with baby	44
starting family foods	46
dips and light dishes	48
meaty meals	53
desserts	55
day menu planner	56
health checklist	58
what to do if baby chokes	59
help	60
index	61

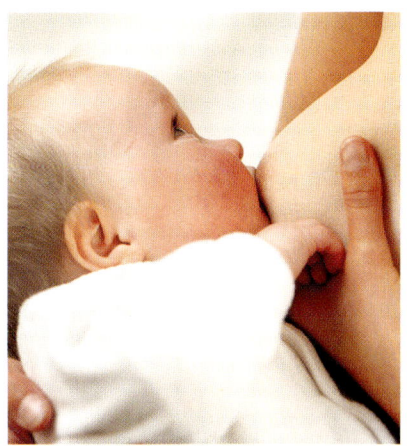

You want to give your baby the best start in life, so you need to know how to meet his nutritional needs. Nature provides an amazing all-in-one nutritional substance in the form of breast milk – and for those times when breastfeeding just isn't possible, science has created formula milks, which are a vast improvement on cow's milk and the other alternatives fed to babies in the past.

When it comes time for baby to start eating family foods you, as new parents, may be worried about what to do. **Baby Food** *will help you to make the right choices for your baby.*

why breast milk is best

If there were a food for adults which contained just the right amount of all the ingredients needed for perfect nutrition and which changed with and during every meal, a food which was always delivered at the right temperature in a warm, friendly environment and also provided antibodies against certain diseases and infections, would you want to consume it? Of course you would! A mother's breast milk has all these properties and more. It has also been found to contribute to the development of the baby's brain and to protect against certain illnesses in later life.

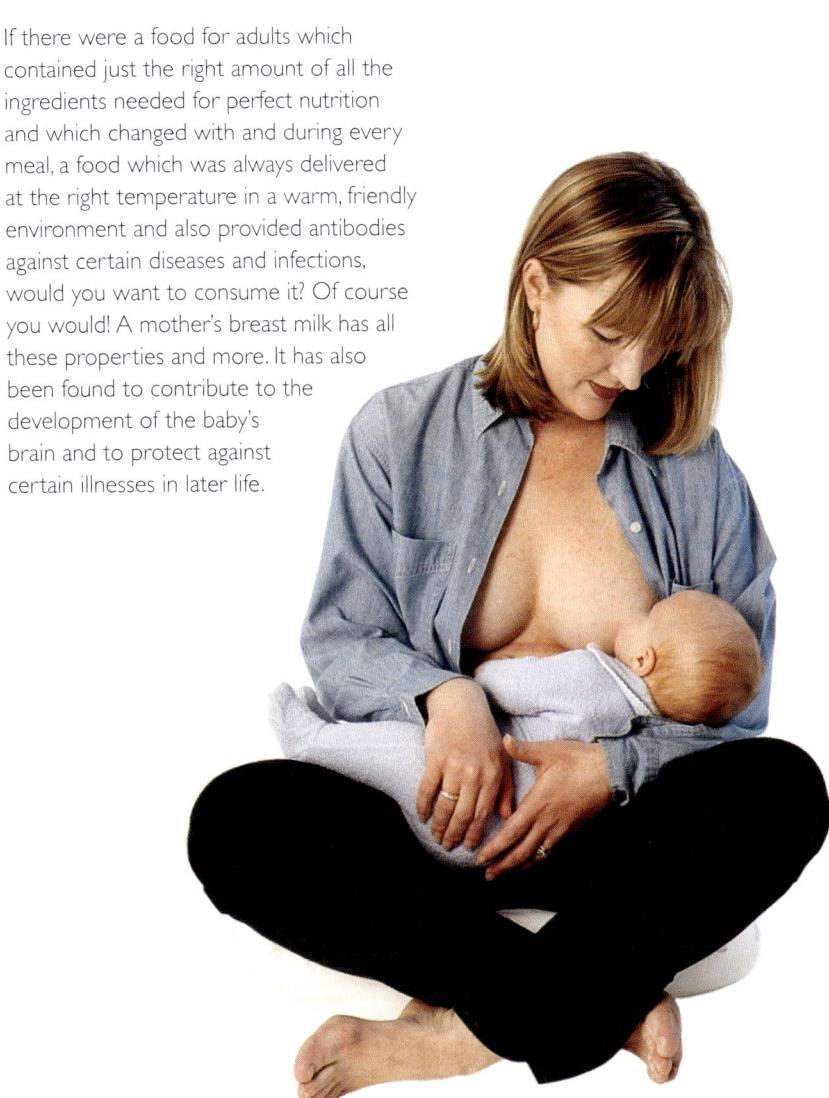

breastfeeding

ADVANTAGES	DISADVANTAGES
Breast milk is the perfect food, tailored to meet the baby's needs. It changes from feed to feed and within each feed.	An understanding of how breastfeeding works is important to its success for many. If experienced help is not at hand a mother can have problems.
Includes antibodies against various diseases and increases baby's resistance to infections.	You can't tell how much food baby is getting – this can be unnerving when we are used to measuring quantities.
Always available at the right temperature, in just the right amounts, and sterile.	It is totally dependent on the mother who, if she is unable to feed the baby personally, must express milk to be given in a bottle.
Contains ingredients such as choline, important in brain development, and long-chain polyunsaturated fatty acids, responsible for reducing the risk of many later-life ailments.	Can be tiring for the mother. An inadequate diet and broken sleep combined with breastfeeding can make the early days of motherhood exhausting for those without support.
Provides a regular opportunity for mother and baby to interact with each other – and gives the mother a reason to relax and sit down.	Some women feel uncomfortable breastfeeding.
Once breastfeeding is established supply always meets demand!	
The action of sucking and swallowing from the nipple, different to feeding from an artificial teat, is important for the optimum development of the jaw.	
Breastfeeding helps the mother's figure to regain shape and helps her to lose stored body fat.	

Breastfeeding is not always easy, however. In today's world many women need to be taught how to breastfeed because they have never had the opportunity to closely watch other women breastfeeding their babies. A sensitive and knowledgeable person to help you in the early days is one of the keys to success. Many women give up breastfeeding because they think they are not producing enough milk, but this is rarely the case. It is far more likely that the baby is not feeding properly and therefore not taking in enough milk. Learning to breastfeed is a two-way process between you and baby, involving a combination of knowledge, reflexes and instinct.

how breastfeeding works

If you look at the diagrams of the baby breastfeeding you will see how far the nipple needs to go into the back of her mouth and that the baby also needs to "latch on" to the areola, the brown area around the nipple. Baby needs to take a few short sucks, then suck and swallow strongly. At the start of the feed the baby's sucking action will release the foremilk and as your milk "lets down" you will feel a tingling, sometimes slightly painful, sensation. When baby is sucking strongly her ears will wiggle. The foremilk is protein-rich and enough to keep baby happy for a short period, but to be properly fed, and have her hunger satisfied, baby must also empty the breast because the hindmilk which follows the foremilk is rich, creamy and higher in kilojoules and fat, both of which are vital to growth and development. A baby needs a good intake of both hindmilk and foremilk. Remember – there is no evidence that breastfed babies can be overfed.

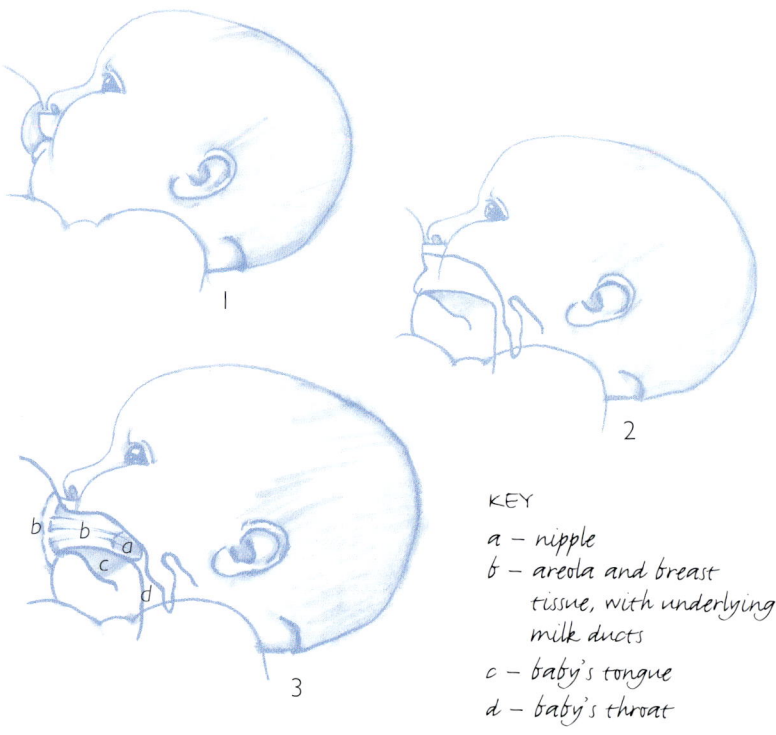

KEY
a – nipple
b – areola and breast tissue, with underlying milk ducts
c – baby's tongue
d – baby's throat

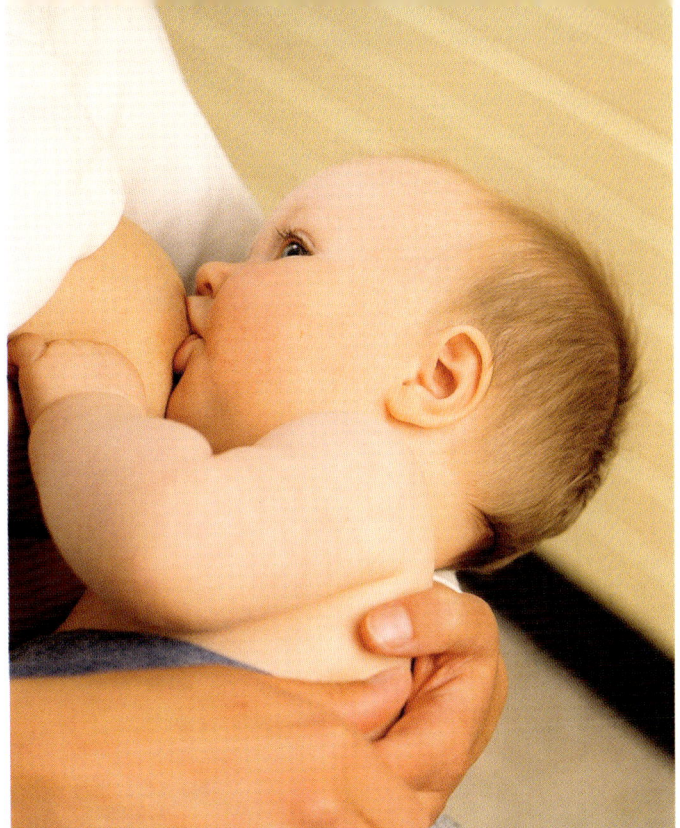

In fact, the best way to ensure your baby is getting enough milk and a good balance of foremilk and hindmilk is to let her feed when she is hungry and stay on the breast until she has had enough and comes off of her own accord. The composition of breast milk is constantly changing to meet the needs – and the age – of your baby. The milk which your breasts make for your newborn is very different to the milk they make for your baby at one month, or six months.

If baby does not attach to the nipple properly and drink deeply for long enough, the milk supply will decrease and you may well suffer from sore nipples. At that point you may become convinced that you are not making enough milk. Without guidance from someone with a sound understanding of breastfeeding, most often a lactation consultant or a trained counsellor, this situation is likely to end up as an unsuccessful attempt at breastfeeding.

step-by-step breastfeeding

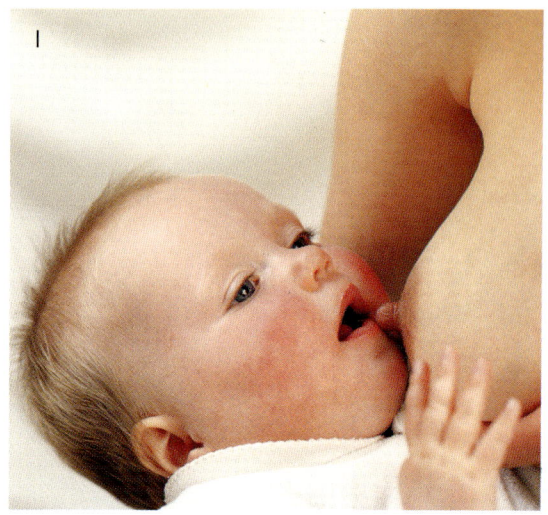

1. Touch baby's cheek with the nipple or your finger and she will turn towards your breast and open her mouth.

2. Baby is firmly "latched on" with nearly all the areola in her mouth. Mother is comfortable.

3. When baby has finished gently slip your finger in between her mouth and the breast to break the suction.

how to express breast milk

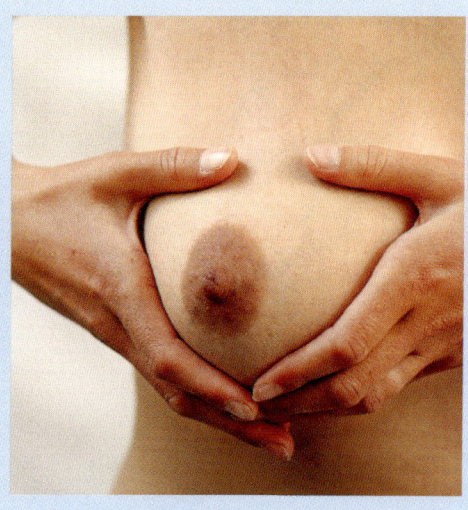

With a little bit of practice once breastfeeding is established, expressing breast milk is easy – although time-consuming without a breast pump. Many women find, however, that using a hand to stimulate the milk flow and put pressure on the sinuses of the breast is the most comfortable way to express because it mimics the sucking of the baby.

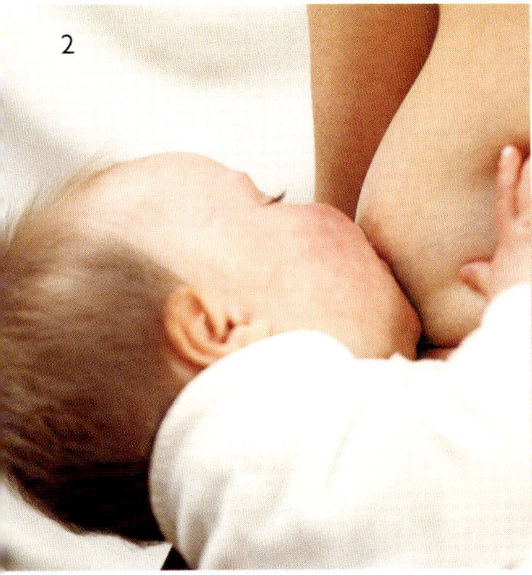

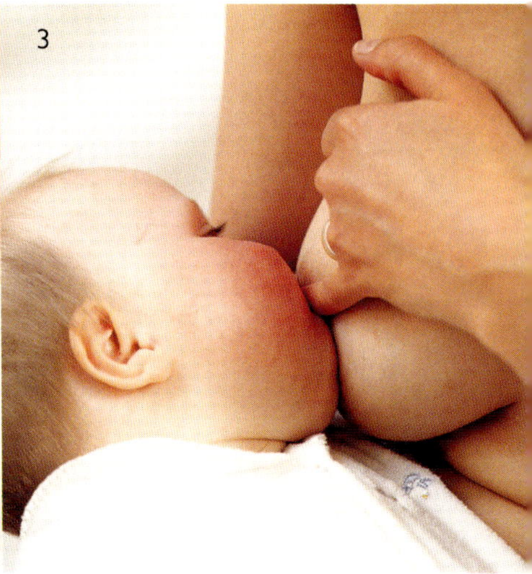

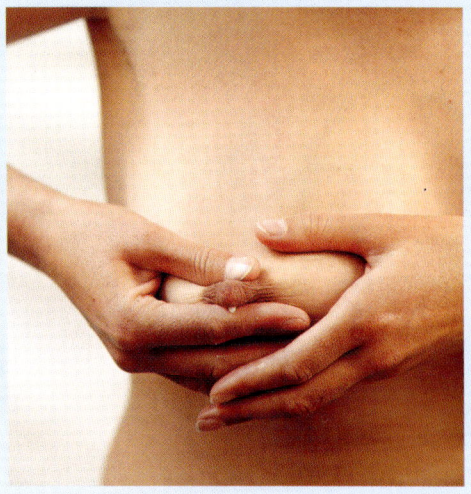

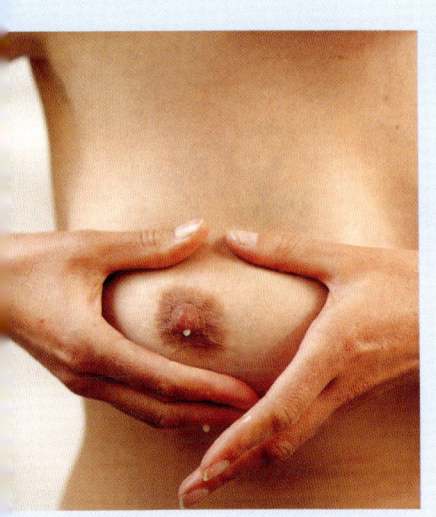

checklist for happy breastfeeding

★ A chair in which you can sit comfortably without stooping or straining. You may need to lie down if you have had a caesarean.

★ You are holding baby comfortably at the right height; in the beginning you may need a pillow under your elbow and another one on your lap under baby.

★ Baby has her chin at your chest and her head, neck and back in a straight line.

★ Baby's mouth is positioned properly over the nipple and she is tucked in closely to your body.

★ You have a jug of water nearby – many women feel thirsty while baby is feeding.

★ Breastfeeding should not hurt; although sore nipples are common at the very beginning, they will soon get better if baby is well positioned.

★ When baby has indicated she has emptied the breast, usually by releasing the nipple, hold her upright with one hand under her chin and with the other gently rub her back. This way, if she has any wind she will usually burp. Before you see if she wants the other breast you may also like to change her nappy, so that if she falls asleep afterwards you can simply put her down in her bed.

★ Once you have established breastfeeding your posture and baby's position will adapt to suit you both.

father's role

Many men are supportive and keen to help their partners breastfeed. Others are not so sure. Understanding the importance of breastfeeding may overcome any misgivings, along with making sure father has as many opportunities as possible to be involved with his new baby – playing with him, taking him out, dressing and bathing him. Getting Dad involved as much as possible is a big plus for you – so even if there are differences in the way he does things, try to resist the temptation to give instructions. Help him to learn to handle his baby in his own way. Too much "interference" may put him off.

When a partner is not supportive of breastfeeding you have a much lower chance of success. A man may be unsupportive for a variety of reasons – perhaps because he regards breasts as having a mainly sexual role, because he is jealous of the relationship between the baby and *his* partner, because he is unaware of the value of breast milk, and sometimes for a mixture of all these reasons.

in the beginning...

Picture a newborn baby lying on his mother's abdomen. His mother talks to him, strokes his head, examines his little fingers and toes, smiles at her partner and enjoys the euphoria created by the hormones which are still in her body. Slowly the baby turns his head towards his mother's nipple; he may wriggle to get closer and nuzzle her skin. Then he takes the nipple into his mouth and begins to suck. A baby is born with a sense of smell – he can tell the difference between his mother and someone else. He also has a reflex, known as the rooting reflex, which helps him find the nipple. This is how nature intends a baby to take his first feed.

If baby and mother can stay together in the first couple of hours after the birth they have the ideal opportunity to get acquainted and begin breastfeeding. However, even when everything does not go as expected during the birth and in the first few hours afterward, a baby will still take to the breast.

Colostrum, the first fluid from the breasts, which is rich in nutrients and protective qualities, is the most effective first food for baby. We now know that feeding a newborn baby bottled water only fills up that tiny tummy with liquid and may hinder the establishment of breastfeeding.

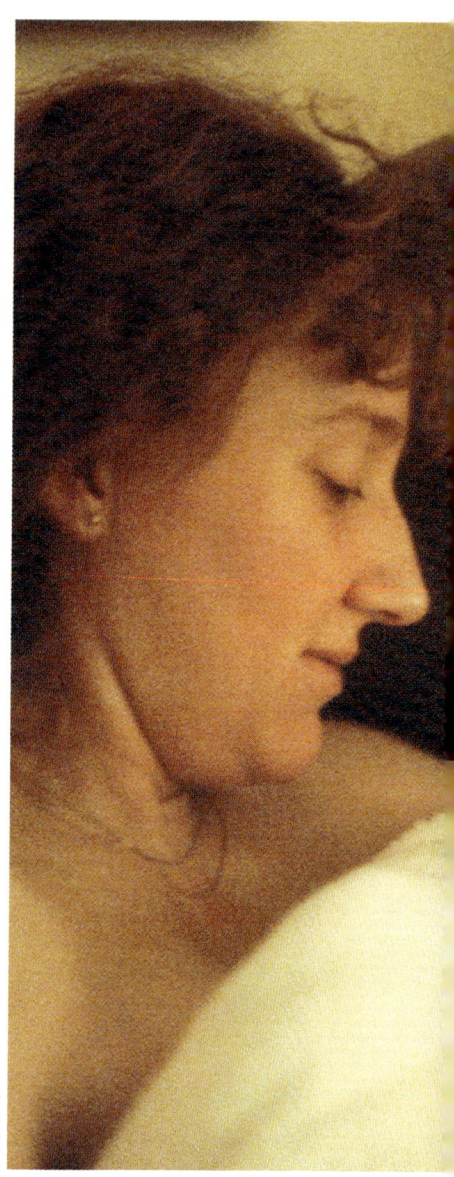

Getty Images

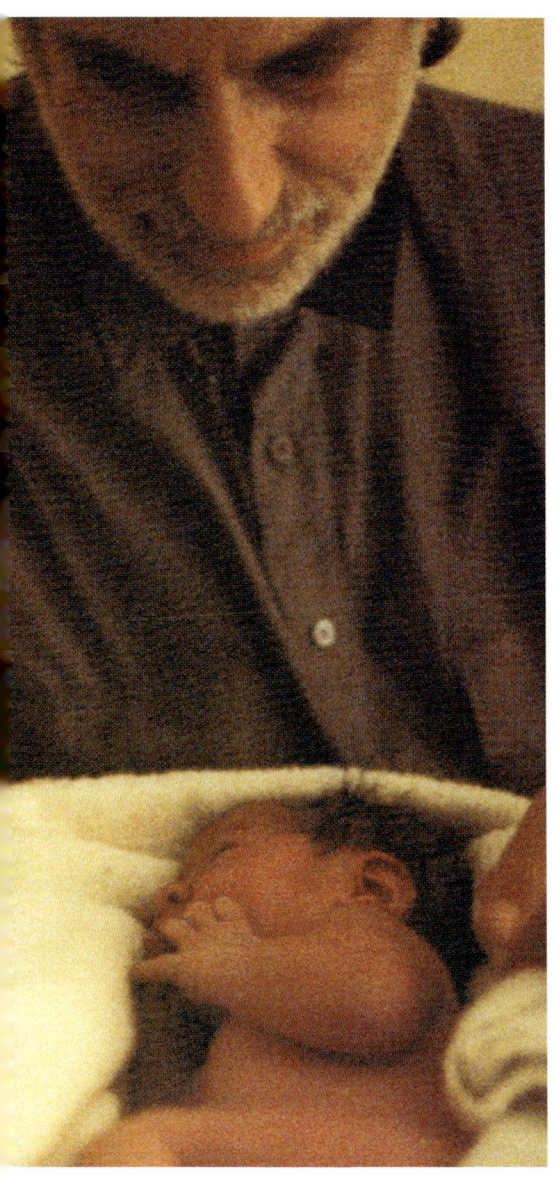

- ★ If you have had an **epidural anaesthetic** you will still be very much aware and able to hold and get to know your baby, who is likely to want to feed quite soon.

- ★ If you have had a **caesarean under a general anaesthetic** ask if you can have your baby brought to you as soon as you come round. Often the father and baby have already met! A midwife will usually be there to help you put the baby on the nipple.

- ★ If you have given birth to **twins or more** you will need help – ideally from your partner as well as from staff – to cuddle and feed the babies.

- ★ If your baby is **sick or premature**, ask for help in expressing your milk, and as soon as you are well enough, make sure you spend time with your baby.

tips for success

mother's diet

It is normal to be hungrier and thirstier than usual when breastfeeding. Plenty of fruits and vegetables, together with four to six servings of wholegrain bread or cereal, around 1 litre of milk (or the equivalent in other dairy or calcium-rich foods), at least one serving of a high-protein food (cheese, legumes, eggs, chicken, lean meat or fish), and 1.5 to 2 litres of water will meet your daily needs.

Avoid drugs, including tobacco and marijuana, as they cross into breast milk and affect the baby, as do vitamin supplements in large doses. Be sure to tell your doctor you are breastfeeding if you need a prescription. Alcohol crosses into breast milk, so if you want a glass of wine or other alcoholic drink, have it after you have fed baby. Caffeine does not affect a breastfed baby unless the mother drinks more than six cups of coffee or 1.5 litres of cola drinks a day. Tea is fine – but avoid herbal teas unless you are sure about their ingredients.

Some mothers find that the flavours of certain foods cross into their milk, and baby may object to the taste, or suffer from wind or colic. If this happens to your baby, just modify your diet until baby is weaned.

be organised

ORGANISE HELPERS

Before you have the baby, try to set up a network of helpers. The people who will contribute to your happiness as a new mother include people who can give you emotional support, people who can offer practical help with tasks such as shopping, cooking and even baby-sitting, and people whose expertise you may need if you develop a problem. They can be your partner, relatives, friends and neighbours, a midwife or a lactation consultant.

TAKE CARE OF YOURSELF

They don't call it labour for nothing! Having a baby can be the most exhausting thing you have ever done and afterwards you can feel absolutely deflated. Before you have your baby:

- ★ Make up a sensible eating plan based on easy, nutritious foods and stick it on the fridge. Make favourite meals in double quantities and freeze the extras.

- ★ Have your hair cut in an easy-to-manage style and organise a manicure.

- ★ Buy a couple of really great new shirts, in this season's colours, which open all the way down the front. These will give your wardrobe a lift, help to make breastfeeding less obvious if you are not comfortable with people watching, and help you to feel good.

BE FLEXIBLE

Feeding baby when he needs to be fed and being aware that every baby is an individual will help you to breastfeed successfully. Some babies are very efficient at taking in the milk they need while others are slow. It is fine to interrupt the occasional feed, but in general make it a rule to let baby feed until he has had enough. Babies don't understand schedules and time limits.

common problems and solutions

Many mothers breastfeed successfully from day one. They may experience a little soreness in their nipples to start with, they will have full breasts as their milk supply settles in, but they soon find breastfeeding the most natural, easy way to feed their baby. Others may encounter one or other of a few common problems before things settle down.

"not enough milk"

This is the reason most commonly given for switching from breast milk to infant formula, yet it is a problem which can always be solved. It simply does not make evolutionary sense that so many well-nourished women in today's society are not able to produce enough milk to sustain their baby's growth. Only a very small number of mothers (around one per cent) are truly not able to produce enough milk. Many women decide baby is not getting enough milk because she is not gaining weight, is sucking her fingers or hands in a ravenous fashion, or is crying a lot.

SOLUTION
Before you give up, see a lactation consultant, breastfeeding counsellor or early childhood nurse. Weight gain does not always follow charts. Sucking hands and fingers is perfectly normal baby behaviour. And crying can be caused by any of a number of things.

The first thing to check is the position in which baby feeds – she may be sucking inefficiently. Feeding baby "top-up" milk from other sources will rapidly affect normal supply and demand. Similarly, if baby is not being fed long enough or often enough, the milk supply will not build up. These things can be remedied.

hard breasts

This condition, which can prevent baby latching on, is more than the normal milk supply coming in – it is having breasts so full of milk that they become as hard as over-inflated basketballs; they hurt and feel as if they are going to burst.

SOLUTION
If you feed your baby as often and for as long as she needs, and if you make sure your breasts are empty at the end of each feed, the problem will resolve itself. While it is settling you may need to hand-express a little milk before a feed (under the shower or using a warm face cloth on your breasts) to relieve the pressure enough for baby to latch on. Lining your bra with cabbage leaves will also help – sounds weird, but it really does work!

lumps in the breast

Lumps which appear in your breast while you are breastfeeding usually indicate blocked ducts. They can occur anywhere in the breast and are unlikely to be anything more serious; seeing your physician for a checkup will allay any fears. Blocked ducts are usually caused because the baby is not feeding in the right position.

SOLUTION
Check baby's position and continue feeding; the lumps will usually disappear.

> Babies who are breastfed do not need bottled water or any other liquids. Breast milk is thirst-quenching as well as nourishing. If the weather is very hot the mother needs to drink more than her usual 1.5 to 2 litres of water a day and baby may need a little boiled water.

sore nipples

Nipples can get quite sore in the early days of breastfeeding. Regulating the length of time baby feeds (that is, not allowing her to finish) and not having her in the best feeding position can aggravate this soreness.

SOLUTION
Making sure baby is feeding in the correct position is the first remedy for tender nipples, followed by short frequent feeds for a few days. A cabbage leaf lining in your bra, fresh air and a smear of the hindmilk will all contribute to the disappearance of the soreness. If your nipples are really sore, an ice block pressed to each nipple before the feed, expressing a little milk to get baby started, and feeding on the least sore side first, will all help.

inflammation

An inflammation of the breast is called mastitis. The symptoms are a hot sore area, which may also be lumpy, together with flu-like symptoms of aches, pains and shivering. Mastitis is mainly caused by problems with milk flow, which result from not feeding baby often enough and poor positioning on the breast. It can often be cured without medication.

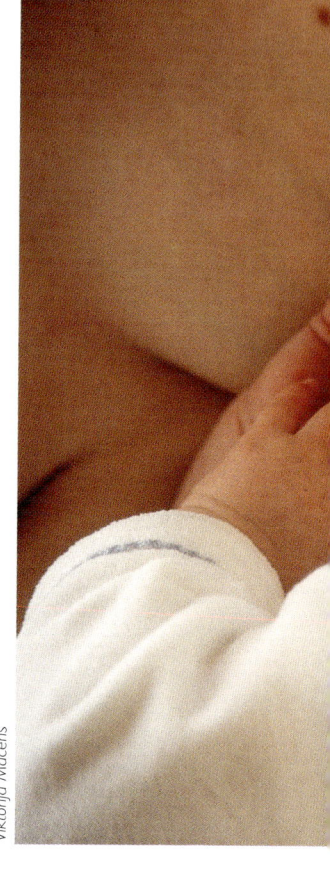
Viktorija Macens

SOLUTION
Going to bed with baby and bassinette beside you is the first step. Allow baby to feed as often and as long as she wants – even if it is every 15 to 20 minutes. The aim is to empty the breast, so express if necessary. Wearing no bra, or a very loose bra, also helps, as does drinking plenty of fluids. A hot-water bottle (wrapped in a towel) to help start the milk flowing, an ice pack after the feed to reduce the swelling, and a dose of paracetamol will all help. Not feeding will make things worse and could lead to an abscess and thrush. If the mastitis has not improved in eight hours, you must see a doctor, as antibiotics may be necessary.

thrush

Sore, red, itchy, inflamed nipples, with tiny white spots and flaky skin, and pain radiating up from the nipple, indicate thrush (the same fungal infection which causes vaginal problems). As with vaginal thrush, a recent course of antibiotics may be the cause, but not always.

SOLUTION
See your doctor. A prescribed antifungal treatment for both nipples and baby's mouth is the usual treatment.

working and breastfeeding

If it is possible to take a year's maternity leave, breastfeeding and weaning at leisure are relatively easy to manage, but for many women the return to the workplace comes much sooner, often in the first six months of their baby's life. Very slowly, employers are beginning to understand that breastfeeding is an important preventative form of health care – that breastfed babies are less likely to get sick and thus less likely to need a parent's care at home.

It is possible to work and breastfeed but it needs careful planning. Basically there are three ways of going about it.

The first option is to take your baby with you to work. This, of course, depends on your job, your employer and your baby. If you are self-employed, working from home, or running your own business, and are able to arrange things to suit, including organising a carer for baby when times are busy, this can be ideal. But – having baby with you only works while he is young, and if he is the kind of baby who obligingly sleeps a lot between feeds. Otherwise he may need a permanent carer, either someone who can bring him to you for feeds or a daycare place nearby where you can conveniently go to feed him.

The second option is to express breast milk which someone else can feed to baby while you are at work. If you work full-time you will need to be able to express milk at work as well as at home, and for this you will need a private place (*not* a toilet) and access to a refrigerator to store the milk. Be sure the milk is carefully labelled – unlabelled milk has been known to turn up unexpectedly in morning coffee!

The third option is to breastfeed your baby when you are with him and have him fed formula when you are not available. Morning and evening feeds are usually still possible, as are weekend and night-time feeds. For this to work you need to gradually reduce the daytime feeds before you begin work so that you do not suddenly cease feeds and thus affect your supply. Even so you may find that you need to express some milk at work to keep up the supply.

Manual breast pumps are available in pharmacies, supermarkets and baby shops. Most are portable, often coming with a handy carry case. Breast pumps, and any container in which expressed milk is stored, must be kept sterilised (see page 28). Expressed milk must be kept refrigerated, and transported only in a cooler bag. It separates easily, but this does not mean it has passed its use-by date. Generally it will keep for up to 24 hours in the refrigerator, two weeks in the freezer compartment of the fridge, and up to three months in a separate freezer. Once defrosted – always do this in the fridge – it must be used within 12 hours.

wind or colic and how to deal with it

Colic is excessive crying (more than three hours a day, three days a week, is one definition) and an appearance of tummy pain. It is nerve-racking, particularly if you have an unsympathetic doctor, as there are some who do not believe it is a problem.

Possible causes are:

★ Hunger. Baby may be going through a growth spurt and in need of more food; this will usually happen just when you think you've got her into a routine around the six or 12 week mark.

★ Heartburn, possibly caused by gastric oesophageal reflux. If your baby is "sicky", talk to your doctor about this condition.

- Swallowing too much wind. This can happen if baby is ravenous or the milk is flowing too fast. If your milk is fast-flowing, try feeding lying down or sit baby up on your lap and support her with a cushion or your leg.

- Over-tiredness. Babies can get over-tired, particularly when there are lots of visitors or the day is unsettled. Feeding in a quiet room, gently rocking or putting baby in a sling may help.

- You are over-tired. Broken sleep is a great recipe for not coping. Have baby sleep in your room and near your bed so you don't have to get up to feed. Or better still, express some milk and take a night off or sleep for half a day while someone else looks after baby for you.

- Baby may be ill. A urinary tract infection is sometimes mistaken for colic. If you suspect an illness see your doctor – it may be unnecessary but it will set your mind at rest.

Don't be alarmed if:

- Your baby brings up milk after a feed. Some babies do this after every feed – in small or what seems like quite large amounts; others rarely, others never. Some babies suffer from a condition known as gastric oesophageal reflux which causes them to bring up milk quite violently – these babies need special care. If your baby is simply regurgitating or "possetting", just be sure to have a spare nappy or towel handy to protect yourself and be assured that baby will grow out of it. If it gets worse, or baby is losing weight, see your doctor.

- Your baby has greenish-black motions in his first dirty nappy; this is known as meconium and is passed by every newborn in the first few days.

- Your breastfed baby has explosive frequent motions, which may be cream, bright yellow or green and smell of sour milk – this is normal.

- Your bottle-fed baby has different stools to a breastfed baby. His will be browner and smellier and he is more likely to suffer from constipation; these stools are usually firmer and drier than those of a breastfed baby.

- Your baby gets hiccups. This is quite normal as the muscles needed for breathing grow and develop.

weaning from the breast

Any breastfeeding is better for baby than no breastfeeding at all. Baby will benefit greatly from being breastfed for the first six months, and continuing to 12 months is now known to have additional long-term benefits. Ideally, after baby-led breastfeeding comes baby-led weaning (which can happen any time after four months). By the time baby is six months old he will need nutrients additional to those in his mother's milk.

Gradual weaning is the best way for both of you. Your body has to adjust to supplying less, while baby has to adjust to feeding a different way. Going slowly makes the adjustment easier for both of you, and also lessens the risk of mastitis or breast lumps occurring. It also helps if you want to be left with some cleavage! Slow weaning leaves more fatty tissue. If baby has been sick or distressed, delay weaning until he feels better.

Begin weaning by eliminating just one feed a day, replacing it with a drink from a cup or a bottle (which most babies can hold from around six or seven months). Choose the feed when you have the least milk, usually the end-of-day feed. After three or four days cut out a second feed, a third three or four days later. If you have to wean more quickly than this, begin by alternating breastfeeds with bottle-feeds. Express enough milk to prevent engorgement between feeds, but not enough to empty your breasts, and keep an eye out for any lumps.

from breast to bottle

If you stop breastfeeding before your baby is seven or eight months old you will generally have to wean him onto a bottle. Some seven-month-old babies can be weaned straight onto a cup, but many still need the comfort of sucking. Weaning from breast to bottle is best done gradually, just as described above.

Remember that:

★ Baby must learn a new way of sucking. Sucking from a teat is completely different to sucking from a nipple.

★ Baby's digestion needs time to adjust to the new milk.

★ You need time to assess the effect of formula on your baby; too sudden a change can lead to tummy upsets; allergies occasionally occur.

comparison of milks

	NEWBORN	TO 6 MONTHS	TO 9 MONTHS	TO 12 MONTHS	TO 18 MONTHS	TO 5 YEARS
Breast milk Best choice nutritionally, contains all the fluid baby needs, plus antibodies and other properties.	✔	✔	✔	✔	Can continue if mother and child desire.	
Infant formula Artificial milk made from cow's, goat's or soy bean milk, modified to resemble breast milk as closely as possible. Careful preparation and good hygiene essential.	✔	✔	✔	✔	Can be continued if desired.	
Follow-on formula Animal milk which has been modified for babies over six months. Careful preparation and good hygiene essential.	✘	✘	✔	✔	Can be continued if desired: 500ml is recommended daily amount.	
Unmodified cow's milk Full-cream or whole cow's milk. Low-fat and other modified varieties are not suitable.		✘	✘	In foods in addition to other milk; use only if pasteurised. Cow's milk is low in iron. Unpasteurised milk can cause internal bleeding.	Same as to 9 months	500ml is recommended daily amount of milk, or equivalent in cheese and yogurt.	✔

BREASTFEEDING

bottle-feeding

In the 1950s and 1960s, bottle-feeding was made very fashionable by a number of Hollywood film stars who were photographed feeding their babies the "modern way". The companies which manufactured artificial baby milk spent large sums of money promoting their product, not only in the industrialised countries but also in the poorer countries of the world – with awful, sometimes fatal, consequences for millions of babies, who suffered from poor nutrition and from diseases spread by lack of hygiene and unsterilised equipment. Today we can be confident that, while breast milk remains the best food for babies, infant formula or artificial baby milk is a good second choice – and far superior to ordinary animal milks or soybean milk.

ADVANTAGES	DISADVANTAGES
Infant formulas are manufactured to very strict standards and are as close to breast milk as it is possible to get.	Does not contain the antibodies against infections and illness which are found in breast milk.
Any one who is caring for baby can be responsible for feeding.	Does not change from feed to feed or within the feed, as breast milk does.
An exhausted mother can sleep or relax while someone else takes care of her baby.	Is time-consuming as bottles and teats must be washed and cleaned after use, then sterilised.
The mother can still bond with her baby.	More equipment to carry around with baby – bottles of boiled water and containers of milk powder.
Unless there are dietary reasons formula can be chosen on price.	Formula and equipment make bottle-feeding more expensive than breastfeeding (even allowing for the cost of a breastfeeding mother's increased food intake).

washing and sterilising bottles

Everything used to feed your baby must be sterilised after *every* use – and that includes dummies and breast pumps. Rinsing things out as soon as you finish with them will help save work. How often you have to do a proper wash and use the steriliser will depend on how much equipment you have.

Using detergent, and a brush kept exclusively for cleaning baby's feeding equipment, wash and scrub everything in warm water. Rinse thoroughly. Sprinkle salt onto the teats, both inside and out, and rub together, then rinse them again, squirting water through the holes to get rid of any salt.

Rinse in hot water and place on clean paper towel to drain. Now everything can be sterilised, either by solution, by boiling or by the microwave method.

boiling method

To boil baby's bottles and teats in order to sterilise them you need a large saucepan. Put everything that must be sterilised into the saucepan. Cover with cold water and bring to the boil. Boil bottles for 10 minutes, boil teats and dummies for five minutes. Leave everything in the water to cool, then dry by draining. Do *not* dry with a cloth or tea towel.

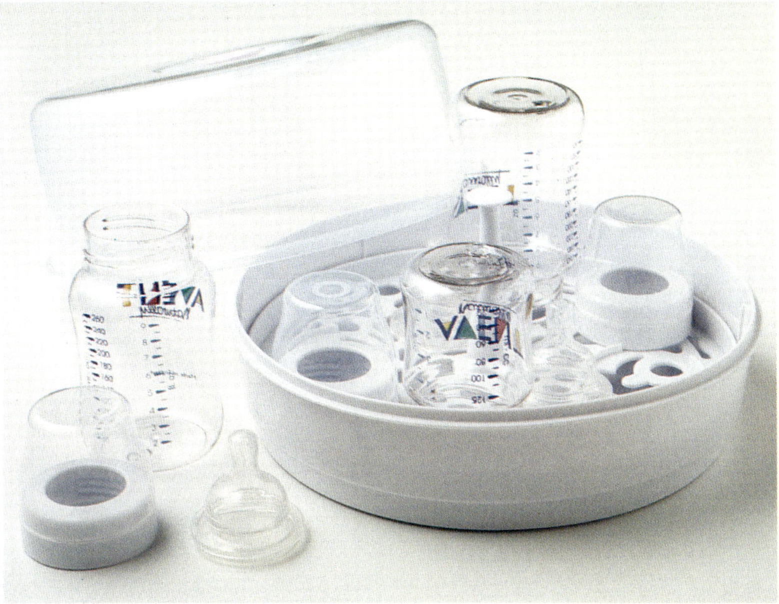

solution method

There are various anti-bacterial solutions and tablets on the market for sterilising bottles and teats.

Follow the instructions on the packet, adding the required amount of solution (or tablets) to water and packing the steriliser.

microwave method

There are sterilising units made specially for use in the microwave oven. These are perfectly safe and very convenient as long as you carefully follow the manufacturer's instructions.

bottle-feed as if you are breastfeeding

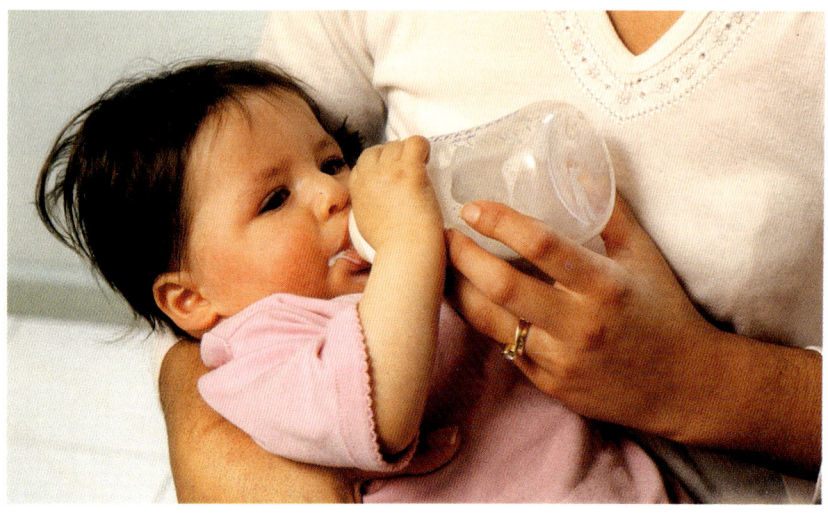

It is very important if you bottle-feed your baby that you hold her as if you were breastfeeding. As well as being a vital part of bonding with your baby, this helps develop her communication skills. At birth baby's sight is developed to focus at between 17 and 30cm, which is the distance from your chest to her eyes. An alert newborn baby has a steady gaze at this distance and already her eye muscles are working. While you are feeding you can talk, sing and make sounds to your baby, all important in teaching baby about communication and early speech.

equipment you will need

☆ Infant formula (one tin lasts a fortnight on average)

☆ 6 bottles and at least 6 teats. There are so many styles, colours and types to choose from that you will probably need to try two or three different brands until you establish which ones baby (and you) like best

☆ Sterilising unit (includes a microwave or cold-water steriliser, tongs, bottle-brush and sterilising solution or tablets)

choosing a formula

Artificial baby milk, also known as infant or baby formula, is based on non-human milk proteins and must meet strict nutritional and hygiene standards. Infant formulas must contain added iron at a higher level than is naturally found in breast milk, because in formula form it is not as easily absorbed by the baby's digestive system. A baby is born with a store of iron which will last around five months, after which she needs iron in her diet.

Follow-on formulas have a higher content of iron, protein and other minerals than infant formulas and are therefore potentially dangerous for babies under the age of six months. Note that soy and goat's milk formulas contain similar proteins to cow's milk and can cause similar reactions. Unless your doctor or dietitian suggests otherwise, you can choose infant formula on price.

preparing formula

1 Pour required amount of cool boiled water into the bottle

2 Measure required amount of formula in the scoop provided, level off with a knife

3 Add formula to the water, put disc and ring on bottle and shake until formula is completely dissolved

first foods

Some time between his fourth and seventh month your baby will get to the stage where he is ready for more than a liquid diet.
He needs to be physically able to take in solid food. This means he must have good head control (which usually happens between 16 and 20 weeks) and the tongue-thrust reflex must have disappeared. While baby still has this reflex, any solids put on his tongue will just come straight out again!

Baby also needs to be interested in food. If you sit him on your lap while you are eating he will soon let you know. Sometimes he may seem as though he is not completely satisfied by his milk and be unsettled. (Unfortunately, starting solids has not been found to help babies sleep more like adults!)

Begin by offering up to a tablespoon of a single food. This is very often rice cereal but can just as easily be banana or pureed stewed apple, pear, potato, pumpkin or carrot. Because both breast milk and infant formula contain all the nutrients your baby needs, your choice of food at this time is not nutritionally important. Don't offer fruit juice too early, however, as it can have a detrimental effect, replacing milk intake and causing diarrhoea.

After a day or two getting used to the first food, try another one, then introduce another new food every two or three days until baby has sampled a range of foods and is eating three mini meals a day. If baby dislikes a particular taste, wait a few days and try again, or mix it with a food he likes.

Once he is around seven months old and accepting cereal and a variety of pureed vegetables and fruit, you can start him on other foods, as suggested in the chart on the next two pages.

Your aim is to give your baby nutritious food and to educate him with healthy tastes, including water (boiled) as a drink.

vitamin supplements

There is growing concern amongst health professionals that we are raising a nation of pill-poppers by using vitamin supplements to safeguard our children's dietary intake. Babies and children do not need supplements if they are breastfed or formula-fed and eating a range of foods from each of the food groups once they begin family foods. If you are concerned about your child's nutrition ask your doctor before you add any supplements to the diet. If you live in an area where the water is not fluoridated, ask your dentist about this supplement. Remember – too much of a nutrient can often be as harmful as too little.

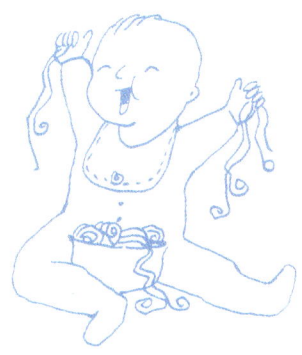

foods in the first year

	4 TO 6 MONTHS	6 TO 9 MONTHS	9 TO 12 MONTHS	FOODS TO AVOID
Cereals, bread and pasta	Rice cereal, bread crusts, unbuttered toast, rusks, rice cakes	Oats, baby muesli, low-sugar cereals such as wheatflake biscuits	Crumpets, pancakes, muffins, pikelets, pasta	High fibre foods such as bran; sweet biscuits and pastries
Vegetables	Root vegetables, e.g. potato, pumpkin, sweet potato, carrot	Beans, broccoli, zucchini, leafy green vegies, capsicum, mushrooms	Chopped cooked vegetables or raw soft ones	Chips and fried foods
Fruit	Banana, apple, pear, avocado, pawpaw, melon	Peach, mango, citrus, sultanas, canned pie-pack fruit (no added sugar)	Fruit chopped or cut in wedges, seedless grapes, blueberries, dried fruits	Strawberries and fruit with small pips or seeds
Dairy food	Use baby's usual milk (breast or formula) to make up purees, cereals, etc.	Full-cream yogurt, fromage frais, cottage cheese; boiled cow's milk in cooked foods such as custard	Rice and sago puddings, butter, cream and ice-cream in small quantities	Rich soft cheeses, strong cheeses, blue cheeses
Meat		Mashed minced meats (lamb, pork, beef) cooked slowly till very tender	Strips of tender meat, lamb's fry and brains, smooth bones to gnaw on	Fatty meats, salamis and other processed meats

BABY FOOD

	4 TO 6 MONTHS	6 TO 9 MONTHS	9 TO 12 MONTHS	FOODS TO AVOID
Chicken		Mashed, minced chicken		Bones, such as wishbone
Fish		Thin flaky boneless fish	Canned fish, e.g. well-drained tuna	Battered fish, shellfish
Eggs		Yolk only	Gradually include whole cooked egg in dishes such as omelette	
Lentils and pulses		Mashed, cooked or canned lentils or beans, tofu (unsalted)	Baked beans	
Seeds and nuts			Smooth nut pastes such as tahini or peanut	Whole nuts of any kind are a choking hazard; avoid crunchy nut pastes

FIRST FOODS

what to expect

The move from drinking to eating is quite a big one and baby has to learn how to eat. As well as learning about new tastes, baby has to get used to various textures (pureed, lumpy, mashed and chopped foods). By 12 months baby should be eating a wide variety of mashed and coarsely chopped foods – even if he has no teeth! It can become a battle in the second year to get children to accept food of a lumpier consistency if they have eaten only purees for some months. Babies start to chew by the time they are around seven months, teeth or no teeth, and they can easily handle mash and soft lumps with their gums.

From nine months baby needs to be learning how to drink from a cup. He will be able to swallow from a cup somewhere between the ages of six and eight months if you hold it for him. By 12 months he will be able to hold a cup himself and drink from it. If he still has a bottle, alternate it with the cup so that by 18 months the bottle will no longer be needed.

take care!

Teaching baby to eat is a learning experience for you both.

Hygiene in the preparation of food for this age group is particularly important. Always wash your hands before preparing any foods, and keep utensils clean. It is wise to sterilise bottles, teats and spoons up until baby's first birthday; bowls and other implements can be washed in the dishwasher.

Choking on solid foods is always a possibility, so always supervise baby when he is eating. (See page 58.)

Whenever baby sits in his high chair he should wear his safety harness.

food intolerance and allergies

It can seem easy to blame food intolerance or allergy when your baby is unwell. It is important to remember, however, that there is much that we do not know about these problems and that eliminating foods from your child's diet, except under specialist advice, could lead to nutritional deficiency.

A reaction to food that is not caused by the immune system is known as food intolerance. An exaggerated response from the nervous system that may result in asthma, eczema, hives or hay fever is a food allergy.

The cause of allergy can generally be detected by the appropriate blood or skin tests. Reducing or eliminating foods such as milk or wheat from a baby's diet can delay baby's growth, as well as creating the problems of providing a special diet, so before you take these steps visit your family doctor. A referral to a specialist or a hospital allergy clinic may be necessary.

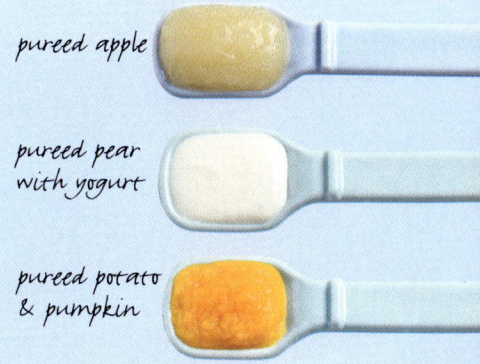

pureed apple

pureed pear with yogurt

pureed potato & pumpkin

nutritional sense

Since babies don't know about high-sugar, high-fat foods such as soft drinks, sweets, potato crisps and pastries, they won't feel deprived if they are not included in their diet and they do not see you eating them; children will find out about these foods soon enough when they go to preschool or start going to parties.

★ Full-cream milk and dairy products (not skim or modified) are recommended until a child is five years old. Unpasteurised and low-fat products are also not suitable.

★ Very high-fibre foods such as bran are not recommended in any quantity, as they can hinder the absorption of iron.

★ Sugar and salt are unnecessary. What tastes bland to us will be flavoursome to a baby who has thousands more taste buds than an adult (we lose taste buds throughout life).

★ Honey should not be given, as it can contain a poisonous organism which causes botulism. The organism is not destroyed by heating or processing.

★ Calcium is an important element in the diet and calcium-rich foods should be included every day.

★ Breads, cereals, vegetables and fruits should form the bulk of the diet for all the family, including baby.

★ Vegetarian babies need balanced diets – egg, dairy and vegetable proteins (pulses, lentils) and vitamin C-rich foods are important. A vegan diet is not recommended for babies or small children except under medical supervision.

★ Commercial baby foods are ideal as occasional meals, especially when you are on the go. They do not contain

BABY FOOD

preservatives and are as nutritious as a well-prepared home-made meal. They can be more expensive and, because their consistency does not change much, are not recommended as everyday meals.

★ Alcohol must never be given to babies or children, as it can cause severe damage to their digestive systems.

★ After milk, water is the ideal drink. Soft drinks are never appropriate; neither are tea and coffee. Dilute fruit juice 50:50 with boiled water. Save cordials until your child is older and give only occasionally.

★ Bottled mineral water is not suitable. It is not sterile and is often high in minerals including sodium.

★ Blackcurrant and and rose-hip cordials are high in sugar and are no longer recommended as baby foods. A diet rich in fruit and vegetables will provide sufficient vitamin C.

mess control

Children need to learn to feed themselves. It can be a very messy business! If you steel yourself to accept this fact, and protect baby with a bib, yourself with old clothes or an apron, and the floor with newspaper or a mat, it will be less of a hassle. Keep reminding yourself that this is an important learning experience for your baby – it helps make the mess less of a worry.

You can sometimes cut down some of the mess by using two spoons – give one to baby and feed him alternate spoonfuls yourself. A baby who becomes really determined to do it all on his own may not accept this arrangement, however.

Remember – food battles don't have winners!

cups and plates, bottles, bowls and more

A high chair or a hook-on chair for a solid table or bench will make feeding baby easier. You could also consider:

★ A blender will make the preparation of purees easier, but pushing food through a sieve will give the same result, as will a mouli.

★ Bibs – pull-on bibs or bibs with Velcro fasteners are easier to deal with than the old-fashioned tie-up variety. Some people like hard plastic bibs with food-catchers.

★ Face cloths – a good supply of these will never go astray; have a warm one nearby at meal-times.

★ Plastic or stainless steel bowls and plates are the safest. You can buy all sorts of fancy bowls, some with suction cups on the bottom, others which hold hot water to keep the food warm. They have a limited life as baby soon grows out of them.

★ A plastic cup with two handles – go for the spill-proof variety if you hate mess.

★ At least two smooth plastic spoons – one for baby, one for you.

★ Little plastic pots with lids for storing or freezing baby food, to send baby's lunch to daycare, or to take on outings.

★ Baby cutlery designed for little hands makes a good first birthday present.

MESS CONTROL

eating out with baby

Taking baby to a restaurant can be a once-in-a-lifetime, never-to-be-repeated experience unless you choose the restaurant carefully! Babies don't want to sit in high chairs for ages while adults talk, and the novelty of a new environment soon wears off.

Even the best-behaved baby can turn some head waiters into monsters. Fast food chains aside, the best choices are restaurants from family-friendly cultures – Italian, Greek, Chinese and Vietnamese, for example. When you book:

- ★ Ask if the restaurant has a high chair and whether they welcome babies.

- ★ Don't ask for a bottle to be warmed unless you are sure restaurant staff know what they are doing – far safer to serve baby cold milk than milk which could scald.

- ★ Book for an early sitting – better still, book for lunch.

- ★ Don't plan it as a night out with baby-less friends.

- ★ Eat out with friends who also have babies. Perhaps eat only the main course in the restaurant and have dessert and coffee together at home. The babies will amuse each other on and off, but be sure to take some of baby's food and utensils, including cup and bib, and a small noiseless toy or two with you.

- ★ Better still, save evenings out for the nights when you can get a baby-sitter.

Cafe Bones

starting family foods

Once you get into the swing of it you will find it quite easy to adapt the food you are eating to baby's small needs. By the time he reaches his first birthday he will be eating many of the foods you do and if you continue to offer him a variety of foods and tempt him with new ones he is likely to grow into a good eater. Getting baby accustomed to a variety of foods and textures in this first year will make life easier for you – unless you want to raise an adult who only eats baked bean sandwiches!

By the way, research has found that it takes more than eight tries for a toddler to accept a new food. So don't be put out if baby does not take easily to new foods. Some of these dishes may become family favourites, others you won't need until the next baby comes along.

Getty Images

Very first foods are easy to prepare – remember fresh is best – and never keep leftovers. You can always make extra and freeze it, of course.

Some foods, such as banana and avocado, come in a convenient "package" and don't need any preparation apart from mashing.

Foods which need cooking can be steamed or microwaved to reduce the loss of nutrients, then processed with a tablespoon or two of cooking liquid or baby's usual milk.

Be inventive when making up baby's meal. Try mixing tastes and offering unusual combinations.

Once baby is eating three meals a day you can introduce more variety into his diet.

make it social from the very beginning

Family meal times are important times for communication and social togetherness. As children get older, shared meal times enable everyone to talk about their day and their concerns. Even a young baby will enjoy sitting up to table with his parents.

dips and light dishes

Babies love dips. This is an easy way to combine different foods and let baby feed himself. Wholemeal toast, pitta bread, cucumber pieces, peeled apple pieces and soft grilled or lightly barbecued vegetables such as zucchini, capsicum, pumpkin or asparagus make great dippers.

creamy apricot dip
(from 6 months)

20g plain full-cream yogurt
1 dried apricot, minced

Mash together.

CREAMY APRICOT DIP

homemade rusks
(from 9 months)

1 loaf unsliced bread (not wholemeal)

Trim crusts from all sides and ends of loaf. Cut bread into 1.5cm slices; cut slices into 1.5cm-thick fingers. Place on oven trays, bake in very slow oven about 1 hour or until bread is dried and crisp.

chicken liver dip
(from 9 months)

20g chicken livers
1/4 teaspoon butter
1 green onion, finely chopped
1 tablespoon plain full-cream yogurt
1 teaspoon finely chopped parsley

Cook chicken livers in non-stick frying pan with butter, add green onion and soften. Mash together with yogurt and parsley.

CHICKEN LIVER DIP WITH HOMEMADE RUSKS

pikelets
(from 9 months)

- 1 cup (150g) self-raising flour
- 2 teaspoons caster sugar
- 1 egg, beaten lightly
- 3/4 cup (180ml) milk, approximately

Combine flour and sugar in medium bowl; gradually whisk in egg and enough milk to make a thick, smooth batter.

Drop dessertspoons of mixture into greased heavy-base pan; cook until bubbles begin to appear on surface of pikelet, turn, brown other side. Serve with yogurt and a little stewed or pureed fruit, if desired, or a drizzle of maple syrup for baby's breakfast.

Pikelets can be made any size.

fruit muffins
(from 9 months)

- 2 cups (300g) self-raising flour
- 1 teaspoon mixed spice
- 1/2 cup (100g) firmly packed brown sugar
- 1/2 cup (80g) sultanas
- 1 cup (250ml) milk
- 12g butter, melted
- 1 egg, beaten lightly

Grease three 12-hole small (2-tablespoon/40ml-capacity) muffin pans. Combine flour, spice, sugar and sultanas in large bowl. Stir in milk, butter and egg; do not overmix (batter should be coarse and slightly lumpy). Divide mixture among pan holes; bake muffins in moderately hot oven about 15 minutes or until browned.

PIKELETS

FRUIT MUFFINS

zucchini and corn pasta
(from 6 months)

20g butter
1 small (50g) tomato, peeled, chopped finely
1 small (90g) zucchini, grated coarsely
1/3 cup (60g) risoni
2 tablespoons creamed corn

Melt butter in small pan; cook tomato and zucchini, stirring, until vegetables are tender. Meanwhile, cook risoni in medium pan of boiling water, uncovered, until tender; drain. Combine warm risoni and vegetable mixture with corn in small bowl.

ZUCCHINI AND CORN PASTA

PUMPKIN RISOTTO AND RISOTTO BALLS

pumpkin risotto
(from 9 months)

1/4 onion, finely chopped
1/2 teaspoon olive oil
75g pumpkin, peeled and chopped
60ml milk
250ml chicken stock
60g arborio rice
15g butter
grated cheese

Fry onion in oil until soft, add pumpkin and milk and simmer until pumpkin is tender. In a saucepan bring stock to the boil and add rice. Allow to simmer gently until soft, stirring occasionally. If necessary add extra milk to pumpkin and extra stock to rice. Stir pumpkin mixture and butter into rice and serve with grated cheese. Make uneaten risotto into Risotto Balls (see below).

To feed the family This recipe makes one adult serving; multiply quantities by the number of adults.

risotto balls
(from 9 months)

Make leftover Pumpkin Risotto into small balls. For variety, put a cube of cheese in the middle (both babies and adults love bocconcini). Shallow fry, drain well and serve with dip or baby salad.

To feed the family Risotto balls make a great entree or nibbles with drinks.

cheese sauce
(from 6 months)

15g butter
1 tablespoon plain flour
45g grated Edam or other mild cheese
150ml milk, heated

Melt butter in a saucepan and add flour. Stir with wooden spoon for one to two minutes then gradually add hot milk, stirring until sauce thickens. Remove from heat, add cheese and stir to melt.

This sauce has a variety of uses.

★ Pour over steamed diced vegetable mixes, such as potato, pumpkin, parsnip and peas; or beans, carrot, cauliflower; or sweet potato, corn and broccoli.

★ Mix with minced cooked chicken, mushrooms and parsley as a sauce for pasta.

★ Mix with drained canned tuna in brine, cooked potato pieces and cooked diced beans for a warm salad.

steamed fish puree with pureed green vegetables
(from 6 months)

1 small (150g) fish fillet
1 medium (200g) potato, chopped coarsely
1 medium (120g) zucchini, chopped coarsely
300g spinach, trimmed

Remove any bones or skin from fish. Place in steamer basket; cook, covered, over pan of simmering water about 5 minutes or until cooked through. Blend or process with a little breast milk, formula or cooled boiled water until of desired consistency. Meanwhile, boil, steam or microwave vegetables until tender; drain, blend or process until smooth. If necessary stir in a little breast milk, formula or cooled boiled water until you obtain the desired consistency.

STEAMED FISH PUREE WITH PUREED GREEN VEGETABLES

CHEESE SAUCE

meaty meals

An excellent way to ensure that baby's diet has sufficient iron is to include a serving of red meat in three or four meals each week from the age of six months. Just one tablespoon of cooked red meat in each serving is sufficient. (Serving sizes of 3 to 7 tablespoons of cooked chicken, or 8 tablespoons of cooked fish, are required to provide equivalent amounts of iron.)

When you make a casserole, mince sauce or meat stir-fry for the family, remove a small quantity of the cooked meat for baby before adding any strong flavours. Babies over eight months will also enjoy grilled cutlets (they make good finger food "on the bone", but check for bone fragments), mini meatballs and thin strips of pan-fried meat.

lamb shank broth
(from 6 months)

- 1 **lamb shank, trimmed**
- 1 **medium (200g potato, chopped coarsely**
- 1 **medium (120g) carrot, chopped coarsely**
- 1 **trimmed (75g) celery stick, chopped coarsely**
- 1 **tablespoon barley**
- 1 **litre (4 cups) water**

Place all ingredients in medium pan; bring to boil. Simmer, covered, about 1 hour or until meat is tender. When cool enough to handle, remove lamb shank from pan; remove meat from shank, discard bone. Skim off fat. Blend or process meat with vegetables and cooking liquid, in batches, until soup is almost smooth.

LAMB SHANK BROTH

STARTING FAMILY FOODS

chicken salad
(from 9 months)

45g cold roast chicken, shredded
2 baby tomatoes, quartered
½ avocado, chopped
2 tablespoons plain full-cream yogurt
pitta bread cut into soldiers

Mix the salad ingredients and give baby the pitta bread fingers to dip while you help him with a spoon.

basic mince sauce
(from 6 months)

½ teaspoon oil, or use an oil spray
125g lean minced beef or lamb
2 tablespoons tomato paste
100g canned tomatoes
pinch sugar
1 small carrot, grated

Heat oil in frying pan and cook meat until well browned. Add tomato paste, canned tomatoes, sugar and carrot and simmer gently for 15 to 20 minutes. Blend the sauce for a baby six or seven months old. If the flavour seems too strong, mix with cooked rice or pumpkin, zucchini, broccoli or potato. By the time baby is eight months old, mince sauce can be served without blending.

This recipe makes enough for several servings; the extras can be frozen.

CHICKEN SALAD

BASIC MINCE SAUCE

desserts

quick creamed rice
(from 6 months)

½ cup (125ml) milk
2 teaspoons brown sugar
¼ cup cooked short-grain rice

Combine milk and sugar in small pan; bring to boil, stir in rice. Cook, stirring, about 5 minutes or until thickened. Serve topped with fruit if desired.

fruit jelly
(from 6 months)

2 cups (500ml) fruit juice
3 teaspoons powdered gelatine

Place ¼ cup of the juice in a cup; sprinkle gelatine over juice. Stand cup in small pan of simmering water, stir until gelatine is dissolved. Stir gelatine mixture into remaining juice in medium bowl; refrigerate until firm.

QUICK CREAMED RICE

FRUIT JELLY

day menu planner

for baby of six months

On waking

Baby's milk (breast milk or formula)

Breakfast

Baby's milk

1 to 2 tablespoons rice cereal mixed with baby's milk

Midday

Baby's milk

1 tablespoon pureed or mashed fruit, e.g. banana or avocado

Afternoon

Baby's milk

Dinner

Baby's milk

1 tablespoon vegetables, steamed or microwaved and then mashed

Before bed

Baby's milk

for baby of nine months

Breakfast

2 tablespoons baby muesli

1 slice toast with smear of yeast spread

Baby's milk (breast milk or formula)

Mid-morning

Piece of fruit (1/2 banana or quartered peeled apple)

Drink of boiled water

Lunch

2 teaspoons lean meat, chicken or fish, or meat casserole

1/2 cup steamed or microwaved mixed vegetables
(e.g. pumpkin, beans, potato)

Mid-afternoon

1/2 slice toast, or mini muffin

Drink of boiled water or very diluted fruit juice (1:10)

Dinner

2 tablespoons stewed fruit, 1 tablespoon yogurt

Baby's milk

Before bed

Baby's milk

for baby of twelve months

Breakfast

Cereal with baby's milk

Toast with smear of smooth peanut butter or jam

Baby's milk (breast milk or formula)

Mid-morning

Piece of fruit

Drink of water

Lunch

Cheese sandwich or a dip

Tiny tomatoes, cooked beans, cooked carrot sticks

Mid-afternoon

2 dried apricots or small handful of sultanas

Drink of water

Dinner

Pasta with meat sauce and a mini salad

or chicken shreds, broccoli and tomato

Before bed

Baby's milk

health checklist

It is important to establish a regular relationship with a paediatrician or family medical practice so that at least one medical professional is familiar with you and your baby. Regular checkups at your Early Childhood Centre will answer many of your questions. You should also register baby for immunisation.

The most common cause of a baby being ill is a viral infection, or cold. Most such illnesses are mild and baby will recover with no treatment.

But – if baby has any of the following symptoms she needs to see a doctor. There may be no cause for alarm but a checkup is a necessary precaution.

★ Drowsiness
★ Decrease in activity
★ Difficulty in breathing
★ Poor circulation
★ Not feeding
★ Reduction in the number of wet nappies
★ Vomiting, especially green fluid
★ Diarrhoea
★ Convulsion
★ A very high temperature
★ Baby stops breathing for more than 15 seconds (this is known as an apnoeic episode)
★ A lump develops in baby's groin

what to do if baby chokes

Once baby can put things in her mouth she is at risk of choking. She can inhale or choke on small hard pieces of food, such as uncooked carrot, apple, and certain other foods, such as nuts, which are considered dangerous for children under five years.

If the object is blocking baby's airway you have an emergency and need to seek help **immediately**. Baby may turn red, then blue, or try to cry and be unable to make a noise. She may stop breathing and become unconscious.

Don't slap a choking baby on the back. Sit down and place baby across your lap, face downwards. With the heel of your hand, administer two quick blows to her back, between the shoulder blades. If this does not dislodge the object you will need to use Expired Air Resuscitation (EAR) and call for help. Keep doing EAR until help comes or you free the object.

Do not put your fingers down your child's throat unless the object is visible.

The emergency number in Australia is **000**.

help

For information on nutrition and booklets on specific issues:

Nutrition Australia, an initiative of the Australian Nutrition Foundation
website: **www.NutritionAustralia.org**

ACT
PO Box 146, Garran ACT 2605

NSW
1-3 Derwent Street, Glebe NSW 2037
Ph (02) 9552 3081; fax (02) 9552 6361

Qld
82 Latrobe Terrace, Paddington
Qld 4064
Ph (07) 3876 2677; fax (07) 3876 2254

SA
8th Floor, Samuel Way Building,
Women's & Children's Hospital
72 King William Road,
North Adelaide SA 5006
Ph (08) 8204 7162; fax (08) 8204 7778

Vic (also NT and Tas)
c/- Caulfield General Medical Centre,
260 Kooyong Road, Caulfield Vic 3162
Ph/fax (03) 9528 2453

WA
The Food Centre, 140 Royal Street,
East Perth WA 6004
Ph (08) 9235 6447; fax (08) 9235 6523

breastfeeding

SUPPORT AND ADVICE

Nursing Mothers' Association of Australia
A dedicated group of volunteers with decades of information behind them. They have leaflets, telephone counsellors, a mail order service and a fantastic book.

PO Box 4000, Glen Iris Vic 3146
Ph (03) 9885 0855 or 1300 302 201
fax (03) 9885 0866

email: **nursingm@nmaa.asn.au**

website: **www.nmaa.asn.au**

Counsellors may be listed under Nursing Mothers' Association in your local phone book.

For professional lactation consultants look under Breastfeeding Support Services in the Yellow Pages or NSW Lactation College, ph (02) 9381 1972

email: **asmith@mte.net.au**

BOOKS

Breastfeeding ... naturally, by the Nursing Mothers' Association of Australia, 2000
Available from the NMAA,
phone (freecall) 1800 032 926

Breastfeeding Your Baby,
by Sheila Kitzinger,
Dorling Kindersley, London 1998
Superb photos and excellent advice from one of the very best.

bottle-feeding

Your Early Childhood Centre nurse or family doctor will be able to answer your questions.
To find your nearest Early Childhood Centre (in NSW), phone your local council. In other states, an Early Childhood Centre nurse may also be called child health nurse, maternal and child health nurse and infant health nurse.

BOOKS

Breast, Bottle, Bowl,
by Anne Hillis & Penelope Stone, Harper Collins, Sydney 1999
A thorough guide by two Australian dietitians.

A Healthy Start for Kids, by Susan Thompson, Simon & Schuster, Sydney 1995
By a former chief dietitian at Sydney's Children's Hospital; out-of-print but worth looking for.

starting family food

Many organisations have informative leaflets about feeding babies, including Meat & Livestock Australia, Kellogg's, Sanitarium and Heinz.

BOOKS

Babies and Toddlers Good Food, *Australian Women's Weekly Cookbooks, Sydney 1999*

Feeding Your Baby and Toddler, by Annabel Karmel, Dorling Kindersley, Sydney 1999
Valuable, easy-to-read information, great photos and recipes. Her other books are also excellent.

Cooking for Your Baby, by Laraine Toms, Penguin, Ringwood, 1993

Rose Elliott's Mother, Baby & Toddler Book and **The Vegetarian Mother and Baby Book**, by Rose Elliott, Pantheon Books, 1996
The best vegetarian books available.

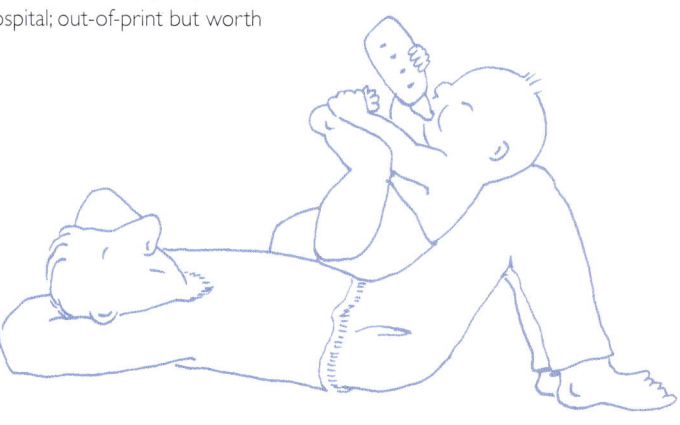

HELP

index

alcohol 16
allergy 39
asthma 39
bottle-feeding 28–33
  advantages 28
  disadvantages 28
  formulas for 28, 33
  preparing formula 33
  washing and sterilising bottles 30–31
breast milk 3, 4, 5
  composition 3
  expressing 4, 8, 9, 15, 18
  foremilk 6
  hindmilk 6, 20
  "letting down" 6
  not enough 5
  supply 6
breast pump 8, 23
breastfeeding 2–27
  advantages and disadvantages 4
  father's role 12
  how it works 6
  "latching on" 6, 8, 18
  problems 5, 18–21
  solutions, 18–21
  sore nipples 6, 10, 20
  step-by-step 8
  supply and demand 4, 18
  weaning 26
  working and 23
breast problems
  abscess in 20
  blocked ducts 19
  inflammation in 20
  lumps in 19
  mastitis 20
  thrush 21
bringing up milk 25

cabbage leaves in bra 18, 20
caesarean section 10, 15
calcium 40
choking 39, 58
coffee 16, 41
colic 16, 24
comfort sucking 26
commercial baby foods 40
communication skills 32
constipation 25
cordial 41
cow's milk 27, 33
crying, excessive 24
dairy products 27, 36, 40
diarrhoea 35
drugs 16
eating out 44
eating plans 17, 56-7
eczema 39
eggs 37
emotional support 17
expressing milk 4, 8, 15, 18, 23
feeding problems 25
  bringing up milk 25
  gastric oesophageal reflux 25
  possetting 25
  regurgitation 25
first foods 34–55
fluoride 35
food battles 42
food intolerance 39
foremilk 6
formula 2, 28
fruit juice 35
gastric reflux 25
goat's milk 33
hay fever 39
heartburn 24

hiccups 25
high chair 39, 43
high fibre foods 40
hindmilk 6, 20
hives 39
honey 40
hormones 14
hunger 24
instinct 5
internal bleeding 27
iron 33, 40
jaw development 4
lactation consultant 17
"latching on" 6, 8, 18
leftovers 47
"letting down" 6
light dishes 48
low-fat dairy products 27
marijuana 16
mastitis 20
meat 36, 53-4
menu planner 56-7
midwife 15, 17
milks, comparison of 27
mineral water 41
minerals 33
motions 25
new tastes 35, 46
not enough milk 5, 18
over-tiredness 25
paracetamol 20
possetting 25
protein 16, 33
recipes
  apricot dip, creamy 48
  chicken liver dip 48
  chicken salad 54
  fish, steamed and green vegetable puree 52
  jelly, fruit 55
  rusks, homemade 48

  lamb shank broth 53
  muffins, fruit 49
  pikelets 49
  rice, quick creamed 55
  risotto balls 50
  risotto, pumpkin 50
  sauce, basic mince 54
  sauce, cheese 52
  zucchini and corn pasta 50
reflexes 5, 14, 34
reflux 24, 25
regurgitation 25
restaurants 44
rooting reflex 14
safety harness 39
salt 40
sense of smell 14
seeds and nuts 37
soft drinks 40
solids and sleep 35
sore nipples 6, 20
soy milk 33
sterilising bottles 30-31, 39
sugar 40
supply and demand 4, 18
sweets 40
taste buds 40
tea 16, 41
textures of food 38
thrush 21
tobacco 16
tongue-thrust reflex 34
"top-up" milk 18
tummy pain 24
urinary tract infection 25
vegetarianism 40
vitamins 35
wind 24

Editor-in-chief Mary Coleman
Managing editor Susan Tomnay
Senior editor Georgina Bitcon
Editor Anne Savage
Design concept Michele Withers
Designer Mary Keep
Photographer Scott Cameron
Stylist Mary-Anne Danaher
Illustrator Jo McComiskey
Sales manager Jennifer McDonald
Group publisher Jill Baker
Publisher Sue Wannan
Chief executive officer John Alexander

Produced by *The Australian Women's Weekly* Home Library, Sydney.

Colour separations by ACP Colour Graphics Pty Ltd, Sydney.
Printing by Dai Nippon Printing, Hong Kong
Published by ACP Publishing Pty Limited, 54 Park St, Sydney; GPO Box 4088, Sydney, NSW 1028. Ph: (02) 9282 8618 Fax: (02) 9267 9438.

awwhomelib@acp.com.au
www.awwbooks.com.au

Australia Distributed by Network Distribution Company, GPO Box 4088, Sydney, NSW 1028. Ph: (02) 9282 8777 Fax: (02) 9264 3278.

United Kingdom Distributed by Australian Consolidated Press (UK), Moulton Park Business Centre, Red House Road, Moulton Park, Northampton, NN3 6AQ. Ph: (01604) 497 531 Fax: (01604) 497 533 Acpukltd@aol.com

Canada Distributed by Whitecap Books Ltd, 351 Lynn Ave, North Vancouver, BC, V7J 2C4, Ph: (604) 980 9852.

New Zealand Distributed by Netlink Distribution Company, Level 4, 23 Hargreaves St, College Hill, Auckland 1, Ph: (9) 302 7616.

South Africa Distributed by PSD Promotions (Pty) Ltd, PO Box 1175, Isando 1600, SA, Ph: (011) 392 6065.
CNA Limited, Newsstand Division, PO Box 10799, Johannesburg 2000. Ph: (011) 491 7500.

Fallows, Carol.

Baby food.

Includes index.
ISBN 1 86396 224 7.

1.Bottle feeding. 2 Breast feeding. I. Title.
(Series: Australian Women's Weekly
parenting guides; 2).
649.3

© ACP Publishing Pty Limited 2001
ACN 053 273 546
ABN 18 053 273 546

This publication is copyright. No part of it may be reproduced or transmitted in any form without the written permission of the publishers.

Cover photograph Getty Images
Back cover photograph Scott Cameron

Products used in photographs were supplied by:

Avent products, NSW, Australia,
phone (02) 9436 0723

Britax Child-Care Products Pty Ltd, Vic, Australia,
phone (03) 9288 7288.

Cafe Bones, NSW, Australia
phone 0401 388871

Oshkosh B'Gosh, NSW, Australia
phone (02) 9316 8600

Safety 1st products, Vic, Australia
phone (03) 9579 0533